All This Time

Wave Books

Seattle and New York

Cedar Sigo

All This Time

Published by Wave Books

www.wavepoetry.com

Copyright © 2021 by Cedar Sigo

Wave Books titles are distributed to the trade by
Consortium Book Sales and Distribution

Phone: 800-283-3572 / SAN 631-760X

Library of Congress Cataloging-in-Publication Data

Names: Sigo, Cedar, author.

Title: All this time / Cedar Sigo.

Description: First edition. | Seattle : Wave Books, [2021]

Identifiers: LCCN 2021009902 | ISBN 9781950268474 (hardcover)
ISBN 9781950268467 (paperback)

Subjects: LCGFT: Poetry.

Classification: LCC PS3619.I473 A78 2021 | DDC 811/.6—dc23

LC record available at https://lccn.loc.gov/2021009902

Designed by Crisis

Printed in the United States of America

9 8 7 6 5 4 3 2 1

First Edition

Wave Books 096

For Brian Marr

*—endless strands
of another songbook—*

All

This Time

On Distortion

(Welcome everything in)
Using both cursive and print in the same
paragraph or voluminous examples of
"cross-writing" during civil war when
paper turns scarce. When the words do
not resolve but clank and die next to
each other. Arbitrary actions leveled at
flagstones in architecture, resetting our
margins after the poem has already been
typed into "emotional" paragraphs. A
hovering form of distortion. That we die
and only the recordings will go on
existing. Who filled my head with such
dark and exceedingly separate stars?
Ghosts I lifted along the turns of
wandered roads, ahead of the game,
behind the times. We regret our early
books for their lack of innate distortion,
a dead yellow breeze onto the gold coin
floor show (molten lights). When he
faints from terror she busies herself. A
crinkling irritation, violin electric black.

A writer is a foreign country coated in
ritual dust. I mistrust my neighbor's
children, all government, they have
come out as a terrible person (in droves).
I welcome you into the sound of
repeating our demands, as distillate,
archive, plumes of coal smoke, simply
the time it takes for the bank to form
above us. "Living goes on
to resemble its cure." And setting that
against John's line "Sexual facts are
tiring, too . . ." I dreamed Christopher Smart
as the escaped lunatic hero who begins
to detain fascist after fascist through
force, shadows of iron lace, Saint
Peters & Royal St. for the final chase.
For I will consider my sonnets
unconnected, titled and dull forever
after this, fluttering after full of worry, I
will keep blowing out this brutalist
stricture in music—demanding a
dynamic in language that mirrors the
mind is insanity, a common distortion.
Where there is no actual clash and
surrender, it's every day and still has a
sprung enclosure effect. *Orange and
Black Wall* falls over two pages. I make

endless destroyed works as they will
become the best poetry, exquisite, half
forgotten, a torn tissue, four to eight
specks of unequal green.

Arsenal 4

Cinders
in clotted
smoke
stone of
the war
and its gleaming
battle plans
reduced to
perfection
the floors reappear
in silent
symphonic gestures,
a folded paper
calico window
hung with tiger
skins, knocking twice
at night
Jerusalem red
lamps
worn more
as a garland
than her smear turning

trampled door
breaking the fall
scribbles
under square jars,
giants
in long fits
in hieroglyphics
the painters
weaned on
bent reed pens
drilled holes, blood
ink of Gorgons
(violet)
sample of
the sirens
hooked
in delay over
and underwater
approaches
replete
faint
bluish gray

Secrets of the Inner Mind

The Age of Gold cracked me up last night
asters and sparrows to be exact,

that unrelenting knot in
the choral fire. It's good exercise, to get out

on stage, to stand in the silvered chamber
and deny emptiness, when the pocket falls so deep

one could mark anything out over the top

the India ink drops continuously
its likeness, still Helen as phantom
not the truth of the state of her body

but being awash in a sound, uprooted

the desk is still a symbol I pile things on
pin down elegies, illegible dates, introductions scrawled

on slender backs of envelopes, receipts, small machine-like
cloud chambers, talon disconnected.

Sunlight burns my feet putting away
the wet mop, where I am stopped

from almost killing myself. All that wobbling of the lens
nonsense, I will cling to the truth of the soundtrack

tearing through the unveiling:
Jeanne Moreau's scepter coated in dust
a darkness poured from the open door, crowned

enameled teeth of *Tyrannosaurus rex*

*

Their portrait is crushed
to the point of flowers

Their lines are reaching
arms out from the center

Their lace is torn over
the image at points

a flame like insistence
flaring this all up from behind

one piss-driven, lifelike icicle
the diamond district through a downpour

past the lovesick dungeons
of Dante, a cleaving after in Sappho,

what remains of a dialogue?
The small, blobbed cellular enclosure

slipping it into strings
letting it wither

*

No god but the act

creator eternally rested
in light

                    fears for my life
dissolved in the booth
                         largely unknown
fire exit back/ of the hotel closet door
satin sheets

light-foot thunder

lover impaled/ outside of that world

cutting young poets

much slack
and the box for the board
missing:

remains of the maze

spit out from a star

November 19, 2016

for Joanne Kyger

1

Poetry is the part
        that no one sees

clip the flower
        burn the brush

                watch rain stream

                                down
                the moon-viewing

        window
six drops fold together
                        then glimmer

burn a stick of Autumn Leaves

                        crack the screen door
write longer

have beams shooting

out and over
                    the blessed
bountiful body

Do not revisit
                    poems the next day

they have already rejoined the actual

                    matter
                    daily music fallen
back into the fabric

          to acknowledge mastery

               would violate her
flexibility

          even further terms (the heat

          and shapc of thc mountain)

2

Bring

the outside in . . .

the gray continuous

tangle of moss

posing as a mandala

burning the

sudden white

tiny

cracks

in between

outside

Microtonal
Concertape

The balcony is cut swiftly
falls as a drawbridge

A secret two-story harp
(exposed) (mangled)
Marimba Eroica
cold fog

.

I lay my hands
on silver strings
it's no secret
I form my own
instruments

an oval, shimmering
kingdom, light
limestone green
wires

for the sharp
rain-like turn
in a song

that leaves
impressions

dotted furies
locks impounded
lined paper
pelican inks

(repeat)
ousted galaxy

headlong rush
revolving the blood

placing clear agates
up against the ledge

liquid forms
worship empty skies

.

His voice steps
over the running
of the bath, knocking
of the shade
in the next room
his reading holds
a jagged sense
he may not make it

He clatters on
in brokenness
as if he were
hiking (in ascension)
citing certain
medicine words
in order

.

Moonscape in reverse
scattered rocks cutting
up and away from the waves

six descending tones

—mustard
—bleached gold

—flamingo
—Mars red
—burnt orange
—bleeding cove

dry underneath

a torch to lick the walls
a singer to catch the song

.

Read *Indian Oratory* deep in the night
And cut it all up

"Looking Glass is dead—
The circular blue paper is the sky."

.

In Joanne Kyger's poems the ground is formed from last night's dream
The thick Tibetan rope is piled like a snake, a young fruit tree shades the long
    plank bench
An agate sits as a stopper in the glass bottle
"The wind is in the light of the sun"
The tide forms an inlet, cutting off a small boat anchored beside timid lovers
The ends of clouds have spiral lines like scrolls, Japanese woodcuts of waves
    spilling over

"A lone hummingbird sits on the limb where there used to be two"
The poplars grow past a red circular sun, dense lines quilted behind it, frozen in
    light, a postcard cut tall and thin
The foot-prints are traced beyond the cliffs
Long stories are meant for empty containers
The woodpile is arranged upside down, wisps of cold, web-like grass underneath
The black branches hang down and narrow to purple leaves dividing the page

.

one cloud forms a low
solid ceiling over the Pacific

two blue-jays swerve out
against another sky

one paved ring (white)
around East Peak

watch the dragonflies
drop off, away

"we visit now
more than we did
when I couldn't
drive myself
up to see you"

.

the lilt in

    "drifters
  at night"

their distortion

(like) embalming of
shooting light

    turned figures

    and soon
I couldn't recognize
distortions at all

their closet, inward radiance
and carryover
was how I lived

    How the coast is not
        my dream jagged line

but a living massacre
a round, continuous ocean view

                all the way asking
of reflection, again
        suspension

        in sound
    means circling,

        chasing down—

    scaring off
old edges

    .

The remnants of a lovely
party strung out,
sensitive, dark-eyed
woodcuts in love
young and old
candlelit tombs
casting down planks
through the darkness
crossing canals toward
the shaded corners
of the house

On the Way

Have the swallows
                returned

    to my porchlight?

I may have left it on
            through the night

            I may have burnt them out

            when the wind
            shakes
                the window glass

                I step out of the house
            hoping for the smell
            of rain
twisted
        and waking up the earth
                the dust
dispersed
        over again

longing
for further signs
of your presence
mistaking bats
for the swallows

rushing up Ridge Street again
the sun sets late for the
divers

'you' are everywhere

it's wonderful and
true
but not location

that's my point
of sadness (the impaler)
no hologram
or talking back
or ghost of a chance

but a small polished box
we can sit beside.

What is left to bring
to moving pictures?

A steady focus
ability to unwind
and rest the lever

the 'I'
left
hanging

open

"watching for the red gold line of morning
to rise"

record the bobbing heads
of lavender flowers (wind off the
sea)
over the shoulder
as you said

"a wonderful density
and appreciation
of language."
Or in lines from your sketches

of Blavatsky, "But of course

this is not the end.

                                          Oh   no."

One is more *in* time

                   so attentive to its wavering

                              her pacing, enveloping . . .

          wanting to see.

Cold Valley

The fog
shades
a smooth
stone bust

then slips
into rain

my mind is
well suited
onyx
shining edges

the reflection
itself

*

Traces of
mist

on an old
window

*

The best part
is grinding
the ink down
endlessly, filling
my brush

gray morning

I first feel
the mind
as reflex

*

Bright and clear

The end of Evergreen Road
is closed and crumbling away

Bill McNeil's red poppy
resolves to be eaten alive
exposed to a shaft of air

between the flower and its flat glass—
masterful

*

The black bleeds out
from his beak

in long tears, ink onto
sopping head feathers
slicked back

black stiches on yellow
powdered eyes aglow

white speckles
      thrown onto autumn
           breast feathers

a white field
      below

Mirror Box
(Dissolved)

1

Balance of
the onrush

its drama one
of silence
over sound,

of being skirted
in passage
with priests

behind doors

color
and cut
gold

a clouded
cistern

jackal
bounding
about the pines
between reeds

my guardians
overjoyed
driving off

the clouds
into cities

the chariot
doubles back
in two parts

a wing
to pump
to slow
the air

a city aloft

for the birds
most grand

set apart, adrift

fountain stamped
dome
at the center

2

long tones
            sweating the ice-locked
sutras

arriving inside of stations

verses toppling out
                    stranded
a river scene beside

        the wires left crackling
pools
    in razor
crosses of birds
the clutch is worn,
                    fallen back
golden grasses
                striking
blue silk

First Love

for Kevin Opstedal

I've never lived in New York
but I died there once while
visiting. Those empty-riverbed organ
          blues (whose chords I never knew)

if the poems are dated surely
she is charting a breakthrough, "large
          black butterflies like birds" and "the
sun is a star" a form of trust plus

reintroduction to the act, dead heat
and playing it off, killing time
          in Isla Mujeres . . . of quickly
drawn and dispelled passage, the shadow

of the board behind the door
          I signed once as Miss Crane,
once as Miss Valdez, jerked awake
the Atlantic Ocean had died and
          folded headlong—disappeared

8/27/16

Six Lines Missing

I lost yesterday morning's translation of Sappho
It was something like

"The rhythm of our fucking
Echoed throughout an open wound."

(I found it a few days later)

"A pain
that we fucked
open all night"

*

There were two Indian bars in Suquamish
both down near the slab

The Tides-In and *The Tides-Out*

I cling to forms (being restless) worried the tides may have deserted me.
Let me write through history's fleeting light among court poets from Japan,
through Rimbaud's sources: A quarry in Cyprus

                    a favorite upstanding

                                             Night Scene
        where of course the queens would run amok

"where you will find a place to plant some seeds and tell your story all over"

"prosody is the articulation of the total sound of a poem"

"the flowers
turn
the characters of the sea"

*

I walk to the other
end of the room
a slender window (no bars)
first sky blue sun
encircles the world
warm collarbones
I see the raven
the stolen light bundled
in his beak
I think of a steel
skeleton passing
back across the room
a sea that washed away

its own rocks
I turned my soul in early
with a roll of the dice
and gnarly flies nest
my demarcations and
illuminations are those
of a wayward angel
sky blue sun and
royal blood moon
balance being a major
hazard of most holy books
lifting the velvet peak
of the cloak over my head
and tip of nose, pointed
down, waking with wasted
sailors, either side,
you will die to thrill
the gods (one night as they
get bored) just the same
as I lived my life

*

The hot water in our building has been shut off till this evening.

Brian is talking about building a saltbox house in our backyard in Lofall complete
with outdoor shower and French drain.

I daydream of dotting the front yard with mostly native plants, ones I grew up with: red huckleberry, salmonberry, black elderberry with dark evergreen leaves that seem small but shine for seconds when you pass.

*

Mind control takes hold after four poems.

Elaine should be the poet in a cage (booth) at the LA art-book fair
or better yet, bill her as a prizefighting Jean Harlow

in a slightly bloodied V-neck blouse
and green-gold pyramid cuff.

*

Rereading the first Joanne interview in our new book (*There You Are*)

"Just write what's going on around you. Outside and inside."

I think of this as a statement on sustaining a variable rhythm within the poem.

The poem is the only hem (the only field?) that Joanne has to land upon.

*

Glass bottles thrown
one by one into a dumpster
sounds very beautiful

though it actually isn't
they bounce off each other and it sounds horrible
for one solid hour

                        every morning.
It only sounds good
if a few bottles are broken in a row
                   (pure accident)

10/6/16

The Studio

Coyotes on a torn paper hilltop howling at the sun, a blaring red stamp

A circular pond with animals feeding in droves around it, brown, pink, yellow
cheetah, bare trees full of lime-colored birds

A wooden ladder that swings down off its hinge

A huge room without bolts or nails, full of ghosts of friends (makers of poems)

Turquoise and black at battle in square shapes and ends of blades interlocked
offscreen

Reams of paper in boxes (perfect, blank) next to ladders leaning out of the roof

Rodin's sink crusted over with plaster, dry wrinkled hands resting on threshold

Seafoam-green door, withered markings, golden deadbolt, Depression glass
tomb

Spilled green wine teased into gargoyle, his eyes are seething, his ears are
burning

Light unburied, unchained

I am leaving to be driven down to Mexico City
    The line between seems incidental

I am going underground in Oaxaca
    to flip through rare European monographs on air-conditioned mezzanines
                Odilon Redon's *Angel in Chains*, Joan Mitchell's
        blighted canary and fuchsia permissions (wings)

In the longest dreams I sail my raft to Puerto Vallarta
    Thin mauve and pink bands in the sky lie still and hold clear like the tropics,
        the equator

Brazen heatwaves slice the earth in half . . .

If Brian and I are allowed to land in San Miguel
    the young horses will sprout wings and become handsome, sought-after
        devils.

I will lead a rebellion through the streets of Pátzcuaro
    and lose my head which (unattached) will continue to organize and write
                and reverberate! Become immortalized in oil
        a large head, wrought of light
            painted by Leonora Carrington

Twilight of the Gods

"None of us floozies was that nuts . . ."
They think we make it up as we go along
Instead of our heated suspension,
precious time resealing the vault
buried alive for a midnight thrill
I can just mistake the light for another line of entry
These dehumanizing times (platforms)
for which the phone itself speaks regret
I will just need a drawer, maybe two, a moment
to rush to the tablet and say a little something crooked
not turn brittle and panic
Shrink it all down to the artifact
You won't need to read it back
to hear where it catches (in readings)
It emerges at once and clearly
with sunken vistas and typewriter-tilted rain
a heart-shaped flame in cool white stone.

Symbol on a Box Lid

for John Godfrey

Earth defined humans
scaling and shaping
this one absence
of a reading . . .

Bridled to ride
through entwined
circular gates

That tightening
the room back
after endless
waterfalls,
stadium applause
for our perfect
zoning-out poet

He courses in
and through
the ends of lines

(I think)
or by sealing
them off?

Jokes parading
as daylight flowers
in frills

encaustic pavements,
our Egyptian
sand

Never the same
hand
on the
banister

Liquid Crystals

Frank and Jackie live
to make commercials
for poetry, painting, the imagination

These are my people

breathing life
back into paradox

The men ride one another
over the patrolled waters of the USS *Ohio*
or bringing an Uzi to an all-male orgy, good clean fun . . .

Starting work on a marble tunnel
for submarines (with lighthouse signal)

French cancan over high demon table,
in every storyboard
the house is split-level
on fire in violet

the burn marks
look clean to be
accidental or abandoned to some cousin's attic

They won't care for each other
so it's lucky I am here and they know this

I have a tiny
triangle-shaped burn
over my left wrist, throbbing
and swept aside
in chronic dislocation

9/30/19

All This Time

for Ed Berrigan

              Wake up

Feel around for shoes

Sit warm at the wooden table

            Write a tower of praises (oblations?)
              in cold steel
type

         in praise of Ed Berrigan Industries, its massive
                                 sign tilting over

17 Reasons Why

            (Now taking off!)

the crypto
            liquid metal
skeleton

still shows under
              patches of

torn

    ankylosaurus

    stickers

                      We once got trapped in Mark's painted

                  side shack
                        illuminations
                  (Back when Jack held the most titles . . .)

I feel much tractor about things now

                        (and *Selected Poem*)

I feel longhouse
needles point
        Icarus shoes

        Sloppily painted plates
stapled into a set

A coliseum for playing out music and
poetry's distortions. A kind of signing off repeatedly,

All this time.

Snow Effect

in memory of Tom Clark

In the day, blood, yet we live by night
In the black between splashes, Jesus,
I just gave away your beautiful book *Air* to a poet on his 25th birthday
Only now to hear you have died on that brick racetrack of a street
Of course, I think of Frank and Françoise Dorléac
(You may have already met)
North Berkeley feels not unlike Beacon
Hill in its way, having absorbed the available
Institutional darkness, you once told me of how John
Wieners loved the Chelsea, whole nights starring Rene Ricard
Or Harry Fainlight leading you to secret machines buried
In the courtyard, a London life of crumbling my weed
Right into your bag, right under my eyes
Elastic, flexible, yes, I like breathing better than work
Poor Angelica, she is lovely as has been noted
Often throughout our history made of poetry or "an actual earth"
As Olson once soared above saying,
The green light's still burning by the gate.

Like Someone in Love

Presenting—Star Time—David Meltzer
and the Famous Flames, lovely healer and
hologram, avenger of the blood who could
read for hours, when the children's faces
               followed him upstairs, the dog would bark
The fire spit funerary songs
               A smoke of tiny feathers
that we know nothing and gladly say so (smiling)
that a prince is sometimes left to trace and dig and paste
asking after my poems, qualities of transmission
               and who had I been listening to? I might say
Lady or *The Misty Miss Christy*
Carmen meaning McCrae or Leontyne
               Price, either way, he was always
right there and shot through,

        wide wreath in flames

Notes on Nicolas Poussin

(1594–1665)

Death is delirium

in repose, ennui as the skin shines

      Leda in Chantilly—an eternal passage

    with viewpoints warped

                in the window glass, the sun

      gains a pulse, contortions,

plague as battlefield mopped up

         his opium addict, zaftig,

    head blown back

    one of the children still asleep

         the other frantic among the goats

      yanking down their beards

       The mothers feel for the strangers

and nurse them—dead center of the desert

The poet struck dumb

    as though the prized chords
              were lost to malfunction
              and feedback
forever after

Ecstasy is the common condition
      Infants are feral with eyes, a dart
more suited to a skull

              The backdrop (hills) grown dim

              I mistook his many tiered wheat-fields
for green waterfalls threshed

                and the ink of the trees
held a dead dancer underwater

      so obscured
    in summer shade,
              it was very becoming

The Balloon Is Ascending

for J.A.–in memoriam

He was living in America, the same old same old,
Setting fire to dry sticks beneath the bath of Rimbaud.
Nylon cuttings from under the archways of Reverdy,
Spirit blue flames like idiots, run down the lane after us
Reminding me more of our final meeting with the great and powerful.
Pay no attention to the man behind the lost wax cast, *The Archeologists*.
He always felt more like an architect, an undercover croupier
Imparting our poetic ellipsis out from Governors Island,
His offerings always teeming with other forms, the factory queers,
The triple crown, the edges of these lacustrine cities catching the light (duh)
His signature gleams. I tried to steal how he switches back
Into deadly commentary and abuse of his own verse.
This morning the staircase behind the arabesque wall opened up,
Further tiles were set with maze and minotaur emojis.
"Pop" does not mean empty. More refraction of light in leading the vowels.
I dreamed of stumbling on his exquisitely whacked,
Private-seeming notes, brown pocketbook in oblique erasure.
Traces of the madrigals asleep, tickled out from underneath,
Days when having a holograph cranked by the Poets Press
Felt like printing dollar bills (by any means necessary)
Come back tomorrow and I'll have forms for you.

Struggle Itself

for Diane di Prima

Just that piece
of the poem you could hear

the groundswell,
and written in such a way, numbered

left in-tact
on the back
of a flatbed truck

amplified
taking up
space
in offering out

strategy with every form
of art

stacking the trucks
and sending them out . . .

new music/new poetry

Survival—courting the elements
(Divination) to be reliably great, what is clearly my job
the impulsive unending twist
in hell, groundswells

     sounds of film spinning on an old reel
sweeping up,
        glyph-like tracks
        on a white page (reproduced)

      Phones held close
          against the light
          deranged pleas
          hopeful songs
          gospel noble truths

Poems that we hold
          beyond our bodies, a joy
          we can keep ringing at eternities fold
melted in the hot brick

        or crucible
        as Audre Lorde would have it

  that longest arc in the edges
    before they join

Old Money

Like death

Riding on top of the car

A cyclops peering in, cage handy

hallowed light split upon the main tower,

underneath, cashed, homeless faces

clenched and bloodied by oncoming new

classicists who are in fact cyphers

gatekeepers, co-signers he said

queens throwing the master's switch

Their powers dissolve like wet paint

to concrete houses dead sky blue

the mirror stained darker inside

occasional spray-paint with silence

and empty storefronts grinning, an orange

light dying down the street too.

(beginning with a line by Amiri Baraka)

We Are the Ancestors

We would still gather
faithfully around
the last standing beam
of Old Man House (1903)

disassembled,
barely eyeing the camera
in our Victorian
collared clothes

One young man
aside his unicycle,
strait-faced

another
swinging a bat!

*

Casting edges
the pattern

    in the shine

it never trails off, when the rock

        is shaken
        rain will fall

*

We are here and will find you,

We will comb back through the sky
for all traces, again

       it is our pleasure

The Prisoner's Song

*   *

*   *

The
    third
  arrow flew
        upward
     and stuck

we rode back

  sun birds
      bedeviled
  the great stem
  its reflected
      words

  fast thunder
hills
a molten

                    mass
        small clouds
                of stones
                        green rushes
        waylaid
                        spirits onto
        lava beds

                        post removed
        stone broken

                        face turned
            down
        to earth

            *   *

            *   *

        I dropped out
        the little hangnail
        blanket of a
                        door

        sun strapped
        to my back

so everyone could feel

I was sinking

    * *

    * *

I dried out

    woke up

sprouted wings

    and flew away

    * *

      Looking Glass is dead
      The circular blue paper is the sky
      We see some green spots which are pleasing
      Are the commissioners clear as I am?
      I gave them a blue flag which they pretended to cherish
      I live in hopes. I do not have two hearts
      The Illinois River will rise
      A single warrior to write beyond without me

Death at the hands of the long guns
Did I say death? Or the springs are drying up?
Find the break where blood runs clear
Through the love you bear your gallant little band

*   *

"Not to reverse history
but to draw out the strength"

Write in the corridor
to be no speaking
Sing in the hall
to be no dancing
Cry in the street
to be no leading
Break into the house
to be no sleeping
Feel in the closet
to be no running
Fight in the dome
to be no screaming
Lie down in the dark
to be no changing

*   *

Are the commissioners clear as I am? The dampness of night pierces my shield. Two dead men push a stick through my buttonhole. The sun looks down on me as complete. I want you to look and smile— red with iron black. With all of my heart I thank my black-robed friends for their kindness. Columns of steel rise. I was glad to hear the black robes had given you this shimmer of elongated nights, left to waver in the void. They know how to die in battle. They are a twist in the black mirror, that river between the city and the mist. We will produce no sane men again. They come back different and the same. They roam over hills and plains and wish the heavens would fall. You issued the first soldiers and we only answered back, seeking air. I have sent many words that were drowned along the way. The wind is full of bottles and the air aggressive, a red feather placed into black hair.

Man Drowning with Flowers

A dream is not necessarily assigned one body,
the general drift of a day is allowed to form its new surface
outlined crosses, upper human figures, coiled baskets, bracken fern
a lamp that flares out in my sunken chest.

The village is streamlined with collapsible mauve steeples
a point at which the line locks back in refusal, audible,
even his signature, not safe from machine-like violence.
Colossal spider sent back up the mountain, turning out from within
what if the path is still disconnection? (dead tendrils) unarranged.

A pastel overview, even its forest comes interlocked
with diamonds. A disease rife with suffocation,
descriptions, distant ends of the rusted track.

A mask we attach to the screen and watch,
the white dots frolic as if they are beyond our control
or at crossroads, blinding haystacks, man drowning
with yellow flowers, pink and red distended organs

underneath layers of minerals. No message. A green
paper edge to the river. A line of madrone
torn back from the sea, wobbling on the rise, at cliff-side.

Starting from Old Man House
(What did you learn here?)

for Joy Harjo

How to fall asleep easily on the beach,

      to dig clams, to dream a net made of nettles.

            A medicine of marsh tea boiled out to the open air,

a memory of cedar bark coiled,

resting for months in cold water
                to be fashioned into our so-called lifestyle.

Clothes for ceremony
        as well as daily life,
      canoe bailers,
       diapers,
         we used the wood for our half-mile longhouse and totems,
                  dried fish, a hard smoke,
wooden oval plates that hooked together
filled with clear oil of salmon

to wet our palates and smooth our bodies.

A shawl of woolly dog (now extinct)
                    they were bred on tiny islands
        we can still identify,

Tatoosh Island off of Cape Flattery where there were whaling tribes too,

the Makah,
            one of whose villages collapsed,
preserved in silt (later unearthed) and how else?

            Which other ceremonies or necessary edges of objects?

            Our ivory needles, otter pelts, mat creasers, our dances.

What else do you remember dreaming of?

A kind of rake to skim the waves, to catch tiny fish on rows of twisted nails.

Plumes from a Tearoom
in Lebanon, New Jersey

for Julien Poirier

Eke out a few more bars for the jewels behind doors. Lutes and harps lay-up to bolster language out from underneath. More absentmindedly walking the room, swishing about beyond argument or caging names. Calling out over the whole wet season, commercial speculations (cycles). I love that edge the wall makes casino-gameboard green—my love comes bursting out the center of the glass, (foiled) I abandon my trap in fragments. The grand terrace band, it's waning finale of synchronized dives, straight to my deepest forest overnight, this unfinished, uproarious music for vacuum.

Disguised Sonnet (on Style)

for Zoe Brezsny

People don't flex
on Lamantia's style much
that's a shame,
a few incandescent devotees . . .
with Joanne
it's always hard,
how can I duplicate
hypnotic, forgetful strumming?
John Wieners possessed
the outsized staging
and drama of Callas
backed by Visconti sets
geometric, anemic,
and later in retreat
Will Alexander is also
a healer of the roundhouse,
a purely psychic (pre-body) space
that aligns nicely
with Cecilia's work.
I need to look closer

and to quiet this
blown-out, stubborn mind
and then Anne of course,
a rabble-rousing
sheet of sound
offered for our inscription
worn proudly
(in chorus)
as the best armor is

The Material
Field

And here
I thought polishing
knives alone
in the dark
was enough

a man that is a stone
holding open a thick
lined book,
samurai
blown back
on their horses
forever

the one eye
pops
a single auburn
strand is found
and the fiddles weep
as dreamers often do

drop them down
one hundred stories
into pits of fire
for rumors of
lovemaking
and printing
their own queer book

pickling
endpapers

the inscription in
Love Poems,
cursive blurred
by bloody tissue

highly sought after
house fires
puddled bronze
queerish, episodic
locked in over
a rainy weekend

instances of exposure
that amounted to dreams
I subjected dementia
to my forthright
willingness

locked hands
showing out
to the spirit

I've already been
sucked back
exiled to empty halls
where several
solid
signs emerge

the phantom flings me
all around the ballroom
just beyond
and with longing
we ride away
the stars pull out

I'm almost
in your
arms

Surface Waves

(*Waters/Places/A Time*)

Larry Eigner's words
    Like golden
flies
    stuck in
a loom—made
      to fall
with sudden
    strumming
they sound, separate
    distinct

    raining
    down upon
    pavement
the date
no
   longer needed
      to slow
us down
     Joanne's

            work
is a charge
        from a poet
the ideal
            powder gun
        a bulletin
            Larry
            seems
an uninterrupted
        path
        from the
station
            bits of
diamond heights

and looking
        down

Writers have every natural right to resist any oncoming system of language. Carnage has often been used to exclude others and often for secret reasons. Adhering to laws buried in expensive books. How long until the new regime catches up to our body? They will appear for as long as it takes to abandon us.

                Ornamental
                    Iron
                Works

Wax Myrtle—island variety

or the Pacific Wax

Those that grow out of the wind—wide
upright trunks

I have totally underestimated the energy it takes to mistranslate Artaud

"Those who live, live off the dead.
And it is likewise necessary that death live."

Hanging in mist
Writing from under the crown of an alien world,
delusion is something one should not detach from.
Artaud often accused friends in letters of being doubles of themselves.
This disorder has since been named
but not after Artaud, unfortunately,

Capgras Delusion: Characterized by the false belief that known individuals have
been replaced by imposters.

Take Big Valley Road to Four Corners
With the tiny wooden tavern and black smoke piping up out of the roof
You will see signs for Faulkner on your right. Faulkner is a paved road.

Stay on that for one-thousandth of a second till left on Stenman Lane, bumpy . . .
Watch out for little kids, jackrabbits, and night birds. We are 504, sharp right at
the beige pump house.

"It is sacred because it is chosen"

just the same as the shape of the poem

    Ocean Flower Aquarium

      Ocean Sash and Door Co.

"Call Vick when you get a chance. There is a valve behind the mirror he needs
to ask about."

 What was your dream?

We went down to buy French gray salt from the Chevron station

Branching streams flow in the darkness
The branching streams flow on in the dark

One of those should allow you to cross over and even to wear the image, pin it
on at an angle, prick your finger. Fall to sleep in the oil chamber.

What was your dream?

She comes riding around the corner, she is fine in fact, elated. Just trying to come down after tracking life. Up to the minute . . . at her leisure.

"The funny thing about space is that it is layered . . .

an actual earth of value"

Charles Olson was a master of the short poem too. Most people forget that:

The earth with a city in her hair
entangled of trees

"Storytellers are the only people who have experienced anything in life"

There really are
no solid things
This life and
its compensations are
of a piece
like protons and neutrons
Suffering is
an illusion

the dead language press presents

new and skillful
terrors,
futures

Where do we meet
if we can survive?
I thought I had dragged my knife
in less obvious ways
Let language guide
your life
and it will break into lives
of other patterns

Bright moss between the lining of her car window

           Orange planet
      under harp-like
guard of strings

Lofall, Washington, 12/30/17–1/26/18

Complete Cube

Why did he fall but the capsule did not?
And why is this considered an opera?
It's the perfect lily we all grow together
It's the unlocked poem of the empty stars
Hard luck, pale saints with jet black eyes
I think it's about to be overdrive
Maroon to green, a neon block of yellow
Masses of mute soldiers, worn-out hearts in rags
Grazing on dead poems, the drawbridge
Is locked upright after six. Nights went haywire,
Drunk at the edge of the spit, spirits at leisure
Wet with dousing rods and the Spanish flu
Lodged in shrapnel. My room feels very like a cage
With its paint-like play of shadows
Its skylight shows green (lower rivers)
Long lines running to hide

Cancel Culture
(the Bardo)

for Kevin Killian

Last Supper
in skateboard
triptych

99 billion cents with
aching coral pink
rubbed too hard over

Paul's knockoff
shoulder vest
a crippled offense

The one that is
just Christ beheaded
a hundred times

Christ wandering
out in Marfa
spacing at Beacon,

trotted out again
upon the ramparts
we walk happily

spreading the Jack
Spicer gospel of
endless Rainier drinking

When lights-out
begins the thrill of
furniture moving

above you at
2 a.m.—I Cry
like a Baby

as if reading sheltered
Language writing
in empirical infancy

You're making millions
of copies
at work

to offer us all
a way back in
past Hallucinations,

Cabaret cards, degrees
Back-alley queer
Field of crosses

Acres of VHS. The quilt.
Anselm reading
your favorite "Ghost Town"

aloud at Double Happiness,
I am tripping over
the entirety

Your own magic
thrown back
on Ed Dorn and Tom Clark

that is to say, naming names
and Cecilia recording and
me amiably hostage (again)

With nothing
to do
but stand behind you,

eyes averted,
mouthing
back the words.

Lectures from the Earth

Artaud's trilogy

in Mexico City (1936)

or *Lectures in America*
              (Composition as Explanation)

Other Traditions

Vachel Lindsay's rickety winded lectures

              (of old)

              or Langston Hughes body-slamming him after
              outside the Longshoreman's Hall

Anything can happen on the road

where our voices have the best example of spreading forth,

              sprung off
loose in the night

definitive dawn, crowded

cobalt where

clouds of gold are spun
and weighted
         (yawn)

set fire to the wheel

         add Polynesian bells
from the morning streets of Anchorage

         The strikingly white coats
         of two mountain goats

      dried linden leaves
dangled down

     the cobwebs
wet and slivered
       between bricks
          (white steam)

The swimming pool was built

                        underground
        at the Hotel
          Captain Cook
                                        "traceries of light"

                double-crossed

                locking down the deep end

        "The listener is thrown
                                        so far inside
                        before any thought is given
                                        to the body
                unfolding"

Sappho

More than a hero
well, a god in
mine eye

the man that
is given
a seat beside you

who follows closely
the build-up in your voice
how it crashes

the laughter drawn
in to stir my
heart we cross

paths and my tongue
is useless, a burn
that rises to the surface—

revelations
fallen on dead
masses. I am

haunted with my own
changes and racing
to transcribe

sweating out
involuntary seizure
I am like dead grasses

yellow, turned
aside, stiff
as a corpse

Summer Triptych

for Tom Raworth

Almost sick
at Gatwick

Ace in front pocket
made to stand till
boarding onto Madrid
"adrift in all senses"

one marble facade
its dirt rears up
against another
ring of streets

our own alley
has crash mats
the men doze off
with clean bare feet

///

A crystal
dagger
suspended over
empty trees
has turned
itself gray, betrayed
in the absolute
ways of poetry

limestone
encased in rusted
wires, a place
of worship
left out over-
night to prick
the open air

///

His vocal has
a tilt to it
which my body
cannot trap
replicate the sea
instead of the wreck

"adrift in all senses"

Double Vision

Dry tip golden
    as sunken
          points
    of arrows (voices)
a phantom's near
         to dissolving night
    swarm
of locusts
     down iron post
  in cross
           of wind
all erasure
     of William
    Carlos Williams
stars unfold
    throughout pendants
and
   no further
       cool the tendons
    advancement
        in splayed
   crepe myrtle

tall teetering
                voices tonight
        how many
plots
        are gained
                from a book
of his poems?
                        dumb
        fuck-heads leaving
no ruins
                a stick
        is pointed
at the empty
                        corner
        a masterwork (withheld)
                        claw-foot bathtub
        extra bleed
integral illusions
                        of relief
        shoulder-to-
shoulder gunmen
                form a cube
scene in
                nearest sky
                        thread splits
        from sharkskin
waistcoats

                back-view
                        jolted
                                off the hook
        the several
sounded-out
            munitions
                        in my voice

Instructions

for Esther Belin

Tape-record the snow falling
and fall to sleep
burn down a gas station
(not so secretly)
Hello. Thank you.

I want to spend eternity worn into a rock

A mask emerges, two small eyes
Three poems in place of clouds

Have a party
in the dark
and call it a concert

"I was reading over my shoulder
hearing nobody answer the bell"

Map a little farther out
attempt to unwind

keep speaking in received asides
play these four notes out of turn

Now leave the room
join the dawn
and walk the city
with your deadly cough
resolute, in pieces.

Crash against the cattail mat
peel back the tatters
see stars
count windows instead

Solarium

Uranium-tinged
black opal–like truth
We demand the end
of money as poetry
demands unemployment
Always in deference
to the received, freakish
over imagined conduct
(nightmare alleyway)
it's the signature tic
the demon guardian
you must slide
past with your
tongue (that morphs
as you age) sometimes
writing is waiting for
a panel of clouded
glass to come clean
Did I dream Sophie
Taeuber-Arp as
a silhouette
sweeping a pile

of Swiss francs?
I remember asking workers
to remove the microphone
from the round room
(big mistake)
which the gallery
may have taken
as a "traditional"
choice, colossal
visions twitch
imposing variation
in rhythm
the forest
through the city
and back
What if I am
already dead
calm and feeling
undivided?
I will have to begin
to make art
in the old ways
to even fake
at breaking even
attempt to form
daylight
or sing to myself

and choose
to retrace it
old threads
of yellow
varnished
blown
to the edge
of a white
ravine.
The scene
is such,
the wall
itself
is torn.

Harry
Callahan
Poem

"The poems are
so minimal
because the garden
is part of them."

*mirror left
in a meadow
of seagrass*

the lights point
their own way
out in tiny

stabbing gestures
(desperate) devil
at the end of

a crowded field
just his head
with both arms

held over as one
shadows break
to fake a moment

the rest past,
cold lake water
eye level

behind a screen
of winter trees
Venus left

lying on
a white
blanket

green intrepid
ferns or standing
nude before

the backlit
blinds, exquisite
doorways

comb the
sand into
pattern

into evening
sun and well-
worn brick

"My flowers
hang
from a ceiling of leaves."

Acknowledgments

Some of these poems first appeared in *The Brooklyn Rail, Splinter, Poetry, Visible Binary, New Poets of Native Nations, The Recluse, On the Way, The Selected Works of Cedar Sigo and Frank Haines, LXAQ, Living Nations, Living Words: An Anthology of First Peoples Poetry, Guernica, Freak Fam, Harper's, PoetryNow, Open Space, High Noon,* Poem-a-Day, *Poetry Northwest, VOLT, The Volta, Poemscroll for David Meltzer, Parallax: Poetic Visions (with Anne Waldman), NECK, Hunger Mountain, Changes Review, Slow Poetry in America, Alta Journal, Chosen Family,* and *Queer Nature: An Ecoqueer Poetry Anthology.*

"The Studio" was printed as a broadside by Expedition Press. "Old Money" was published as a broadside by Gern en Regalia. Many thanks to these editors.

Thanks also to Joshua Beckman, Heidi Broadhead, Blyss Ervin, Catherine Bresner, Colter Jacobsen, Frank Haines, Michael Slosek, Claudia La Rocco, Donald Guravich, Norma Cole, Chay Norton, Margaret Randall, Barbara Byers, Alli Warren, Zoe Brezsny, Micah Ballard, Anselm Berrigan, Ben Lerner, Geoffrey G. O'Brien, Anthony McCann, Luke Daly, Tonya Foster, Mario Miron, Chris Duncan, Maggie Otero, Melissa Brown, Jennifer Elise Foerster, Joy Harjo, Kimberly M. Blaeser, Brandon Hobson, Sherwin Bitsui, Santee Frazier, Layli Long Soldier, Sky Hopinka, Rod Roland, and Tenaya Nasser-Frederick. And thank you to The Lannan Foundation.